MOSCOW
THE CITY AT A GLANCE

D0226517

Kremlin
Yuri Dolgoruky founded Moscow here in
1147, but most of the cathedrals, ceremonial
halls and fortifications were built by Italian
architects in the 15th and 16th centuries.
Alexandrovsky Sad

St Basil's Cathedral
It is said that Ivan the Terrible was so pleased
by this 1561 cathedral, built to commemorate
the sacking of Kazan, that he blinded its two
architects so they could never repeat the feat.
Red Square

Kremlin Power Plant
The city's first power plant was completed
in 1897 to serve the Kremlin and State Duma.
See p066

Ostankino TV tower
Rising 540m, Nikolai Nikitin's concrete, rocket-
like TV antenna was the tallest structure in the
world for 10 years after it went up in 1967.
See p009

New Kriegskommissariat
This monument of Russian classicism was
designed by Nicolas Legrand in 1781. It is now
used as the HQ of the Moscow armed forces.
Sadovnicheskaya Ulitsa

Kotelnicheskaya apartment block
Built in 1952, one of the more decorative of
Stalin's Seven Sisters housed the Soviet élite.
See p014

Transstroy building
This Seven Sister had to incorporate Krasnye
Vorota underground station and was erected
in winter at a tilt of 1.6m, before the ground
thawed and it swung back to the vertical.
Sadovaya-Chernogryazskaya Ulitsa

INTRODUCTION
THE CHANGING FACE OF THE URBAN SCENE

Moscow has always been utopian in its goals, striving to be the most perfectly planned capital in the world. Yet the reality is a patchwork megalopolis, made up of overlapping architectural plans expanding in concentric circles away from the hub. From its heart, the Kremlin, reconstructed by Italian architects between 1475 and 1600, to its sea of suburban apartment blocks; from Stalin's elaborate, Gothic-style skyscrapers to the 21st-century towers that have been built with largely ill-gotten riches; from decrepit constructivism to the architectural trash of the 1990s, everything is both in harmony and at war, adding up to a peculiar Eurasian fusion of different time periods, cultures and styles.

Moscow is bristling with contrasts that are unexpected and sometimes shocking. If a Muscovite sees an aggressive gang of stray dogs grooming themselves in front of a luxury boutique, they won't miss a beat. The sleepy suburbs and noisy, bustling, crowded 24-hour centre couldn't be more different. Moscow's *elitny* nightlife is at odds with the daily torpor of its traffic jams. It is also a city growing by the day – some say it's just one gigantic building yard – and the cost of its real estate has outstripped that of all other capitals. But herein lies the excitement. This is a city on the edge, and its government and citizens have the money, power, arrogance and one-upmanship to ensure that you never know what will happen next. In Moscow, anything is possible.

ESSENTIAL INFO

FACTS, FIGURES AND USEFUL ADDRESSES

TOURIST OFFICE
Gostiny Dvor
Ulitsa Ilyinka 4
T 232 5657
www.moscowcity.com

TRANSPORT
Car hire
Delta Rent-a-Car
T 505 3377
deltarent.ru/eng
Spektr Service
T 987 4577
www.sscars.ru/en/
Metro
engl.mosmetro.ru
Taxis
New Yellow Taxi
T 940 8888
Taxi 749
T 749 3414
www.taxi749.com

EMERGENCY SERVICES
Ambulance
T 03
Police
T 02
24-hour pharmacy
36.6
Tverskaya Ulitsa 25/9
T 699 2459

EMBASSIES
British Embassy
Smolenskaya Naberezhnaya 10
T 956 7200
www.britishembassy.gov.uk/russia
US Embassy
Bolshoi Deviatinsky Pereulok 8
T 728 5000
moscow.usembassy.gov

MONEY
American Express
Vetoshny Pereulok 17
T 543 9400
www.americanexpress-rsb.ru/eng

POSTAL SERVICES
Post Office
Myasnitskaya Ulitsa 26
T 623 4163
Shipping
UPS
Derbenevskaya Naberezhnaya 7/4
T 961 2211

BOOKS
Babylon by Victor Pelevin (Faber and Faber)
Capitalist Realism: New Architecture in Russia by Bart Goldhoorn, Philipp Meuser (DOM Publishers)
Moscow by Karl Schlögel (Reaktion Books)

WEBSITES
Architecture
agency.archi.ru/eng/index_html
www.muar.ru/eng
Newspapers
www.mnweekly.ru
www.themoscowtimes.com

COST OF LIVING
Taxi from Sheremetevo-2 Airport or Domodedovo Airport to city centre
£28 or £50
Cappuccino
£10
Packet of cigarettes
£1
Daily newspaper
£0.25
Bottle of champagne
£250

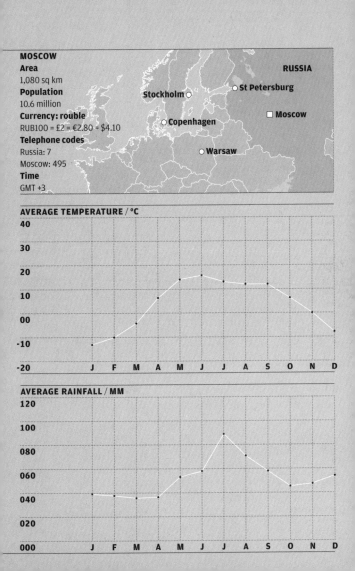

MOSCOW
Area
1,080 sq km
Population
10.6 million
Currency: rouble
RUB100 = £2 = €2.80 = $4.10
Telephone codes
Russia: 7
Moscow: 495
Time
GMT +3

RUSSIA

St Petersburg
Stockholm
Copenhagen
Moscow
Warsaw

AVERAGE TEMPERATURE / °C

40

30

20

10

00

-10

-20

J F M A M J J A S O N D

AVERAGE RAINFALL / MM

120

100

080

060

040

020

000

J F M A M J J A S O N D

NEIGHBOURHOODS

THE AREAS YOU NEED TO KNOW AND WHY

To help you navigate the city, we've chosen the most interesting districts (see below and the map inside the back cover) and colour-coded our featured venues, according to their location; those venues that are outside these areas are not coloured.

KITAI GOROD

In Russian, Kitai Gorod means 'China Town', but this is not a district historically associated with the Chinese. According to one theory, the word *kitai* has Turkic roots and originally meant 'fortress'. This part of the city has always been commercial, and is home to GUM (Red Square 3, T 788 4343), the former state department store and Tretyakovsky Proezd – a mews with the city's most expensive boutiques.

CHISTYE PRUDY

The eponymous 'Clean Ponds' (known as the Dirty Ponds until they were dredged in the 18th century) are sited on Chistoprudny Bulvar. It is a lovely walk from here to Kotelnicheskaya Naberezhnaya and one of Stalin's Seven Sisters (see p014) by the Moskva. Around Lubyanskaya Ploshchad, you'll find the former KGB headquarters and the Polytechnical Museum (Novaya Ploshchad 3/4, T 923 0756), which features a model of the first Soviet nuclear bomb.

NOVY ARBAT

With the intention of recreating the wide boulevards of revolutionary Havana, Nikita Khrushchev ordered Ulitsa Novy Arbat to be cut through Moscow's bohemian heart. Old Ulitsa Arbat was pedestrianised, and is now full of cafés, antique shops, galleries and souvenir tat. The city's most luxurious quarter, the Golden Mile, stretches to the river, and Cathedral of Christ the Saviour (Ulitsa Volkhonka 15, T 201 2847).

KREMLIN

The administrative centre of Russia is home to churches, ceremonial halls, government buildings and the Kremlin Museums (T 202 3776), including the Diamond Fund in the Armoury. On Cathedral Square are the 16th-century Ivan the Great Bell Tower, visible from 30km away, the decorative 1586 Tsar Cannon, the 202-ton Tsar Bell that broke before it was tolled, and the 15th-century Assumption Cathedral and Hall of Facets.

TVERSKAYA

During the days of Soviet military parades, Tverskaya Ulitsa was the road from which tanks would enter Red Square. Many of the city's chic hotels, boutiques, clubs and bars are located on or off this radial street. The Bolshoi Theatre (see p032) and the Contemporary History Museum (Tverskaya Ulitsa 21, T 699 5458), which majors on Soviet history and features a collection of gifts presented to its former leaders, are also situated near this artery.

ZAMOSKVORECHIE

Before the Revolution in 1917, this was the merchants' quarter. They were eliminated as a class, but the district preserved its flavour. Today, this is one of the quietest parts of Moscow. The House on Embankment (see p078) faces the Kremlin on an island in the Moskva; further to the south, in the Park of Arts, is the New Tretyakov Gallery (see p032), which has an impressive collection of Russian avant-garde art.

LANDMARKS

THE SHAPE OF THE CITY SKYLINE

The historic core of Moscow is the Kremlin and Kitai Gorod, beside the meandering Moskva, which were encircled by the Boulevard Ring and then the Garden Ring. After the 1917 Revolution, the city grew fast and needed redevelopment. Soviet avant-garde architects devised a star-like layout, with green wedges between the radial streets. The original Cathedral of Christ the Saviour was demolished in order to be replaced with the huge Palace of the Soviets, but the Communists' ego trip was brought to a halt by the 1941 German invasion. After WWII, Stalin ordered a series of Gothic-style high-rises, such as Kotelnicheskaya (see p014) and the Ukraina Hotel (see p016), dubbed the Seven Sisters. Tverskaya Ulitsa was widened to become a main artery, and, running south, Leninsky Prospekt was laid out, on which the Academy of Sciences (see p015) stands today. To the north, the VVC complex (see p037) was intended as a model of the bright Soviet future; it's pinpointed by the Ostankino TV Tower (Ulitsa Akademika Korolyova 15, T 602 2234).

The building of the Moscow International Business Centre in the west, on the third ring, stalled in the 1990s, but is gathering pace today. The first skyscraper to sprout is Federation Tower (see p010). This £7bn project, due for completion in the next 10 years, will cover 100 hectares and include the Lord Foster-designed Russia Tower, which, at 600m, will become the tallest building in Europe in 2011. *For full addresses, see Resources.*

Federation Tower

When it's completed in 2009, Federation Tower (above right), the first stage in the construction of the Moscow International Business Centre, located to the west of Hotel Ukraina, will actually comprise two towers: the East and the West. The symbolism of the names is as clear as the European-style concrete-and-glass architecture. The smaller, 242m-tall West Tower was built first and the East will rise to 360m. A shared spire will take the structure to 506m. Designed by German architect Peter Schweger and Russian-German Sergei Tchoban, the complex is reminiscent of two sails united by a mast. It's not ground-breaking, but considering Moscow mayor Yuri Luzhkov's peculiar tastes, at least it's not a monstrosity. *Near Shelepikha, Moscow-City, www.federationtower.ru*

Shukhov Tower

This visionary construction has been an architectural icon for decades and is still operational, broadcasting TV and radio shows. It has inspired Gaudí, Le Corbusier, Niemeyer, Gehry, Calatrava and Lord Foster, whose admiration for the structure can be seen in his 30 St Mary Axe in London. The 160m hyperbolic tower was built in the south of the city between 1919 and 1922, by the engineer Vladimir Shukhov, using a 'telescopic method' that did not employ scaffolding or cranes; upper elements were assembled inside the lower ones and lifted with hoists and pulleys. The latticed steel shell is light but durable, and was intended to provide minimal wind resistance. The Shukhov Tower also uses three times less metal per metre than the Eiffel Tower.
Ulitsa Shabolovka 37, T 797 7916, www.shukhov.org

State Kremlin Palace

Mikhail Posokhin Sr, a *nomenklatura* architect under Stalin, Khrushchev and Brezhnev, built the only modernist building in the Kremlin in 1961. Every detail down to the door handles had to be approved by Khrushchev. Built to house the Communist Party congress, it has 6,000 seats. These days, it stages concerts and ballet performances.
Ulitsa Vosdvizhenka 1, T 917 2336

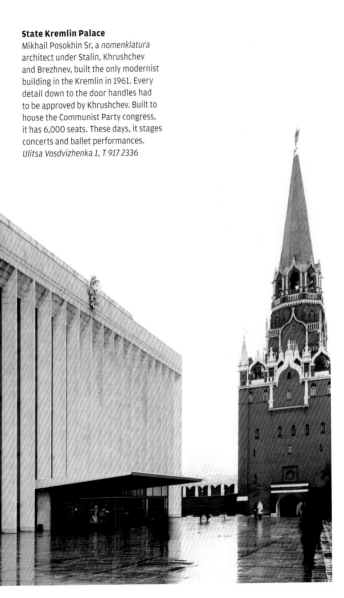

Kotelnicheskaya apartment block

This residential building competes with the Moscow State University for the title of the city's most attractive high-rise. It was designed by Dmitry Chechulin, chief architect of the city from 1945 to 1949, who oversaw the construction of all of the Seven Sisters – landmark skyscrapers scattered throughout the city built to mark Moscow's 800th anniversary. The original designs did not feature spires; it was Stalin himself who suggested that the spires would echo the Kremlin's towers. Apartments in the Seven Sisters were originally given to the political and cultural élite. Today, they are some of the most desirable properties in the city, many now pied-à-terres for weekending oligarchs. *Kotelnicheskaya Naberezhnaya 1/15*

Academy of Sciences

Conceived in the 1960s, the new building for the Academy of Sciences was eventually built on a south-west bank of the Moskva between 1981 and 1990 – so this problem child of Soviet architecture was born just before the collapse of the USSR. The design is an architectural parody of one of the towers from Ivan Leonidov's unrealised competition entry for Narkomtiazhprom House. Nevertheless, the building has fitted perfectly into the cityscape, and has claimed a place in the hearts of Muscovites, who affectionately nicknamed it Golden Brains – ironic considering that its copper-piping hat was supposed to provide solar power, but has never worked due to an engineering glitch. In 2005, the *elitny* bar/restaurant Sky Lounge (see p050), opened in the right 'brain', providing superb views. *Leninsky Prospekt 32a, T 938 0309*

HOTELS

WHERE TO STAY AND WHICH ROOMS TO BOOK

In the early noughties, locals used to quip: 'Luzhkov destroyed Moscow and dismantled Russia; Space and Peace are next.' The joke was that these were all names of architecturally significant or historic Soviet hotels that had been pulled down or closed for renovation. Fortunately, the Metropol (see p025) and the National (opposite) have survived the cull; however the imposing, neo-Gothic Ukraina (Kutuzovsky Prospekt 2/1, T 221 5555) is being overhauled – fingers crossed for its 2011 reopening. The surviving Cosmos (Prospekt Mira 150, T 234 1000) is a fascinating piece of Soviet neo-modernism, but not recommended as accommodation.

In the 1990s, the city centre was invaded by the international chains. Tverskaya Ulitsa now has a couple of Marriotts and The Ritz-Carlton (see p026); the Ararat Park Hyatt (see p020) is round the corner and the Baltschug Kempinski (see p028) is on the other side of Red Square. All of them are reassuringly expensive, international business boltholes. However, boutique hotels are catching on at last, their bright colour schemes and pumping, 24-hour club music in the lobbies a typically Muscovite slant. The Golden Apple (overleaf) was joined in 2007 by the ultra-stylish MaMaison Pokrovka Suite Hotel (see p022). The latest, Enigma WEL (Staraya Basmannaya Ulitsa 12/1, T 648 9292), has themed floors and minimalist rooms in a restored 19th-century mansion. *For full addresses and room rates, see Resources.*

Le Royal Méridien National

When it opened in 1903, the National soon became a place for revelry for Moscow high society. After the Revolution, it was the only hotel in the city that was deemed suitable for visiting foreign officials – when Jacques Chirac saw Room 101, a suite designed to reflect early 20th-century Russian ideas about the lifestyle of Louis XVI, he asked: 'Is it intended for living in?' Fortunately, the hotel's historic structure, antique furniture and frescoed ceilings have survived its renovation. The best rooms are the Presidential and National Suites, such as Room 115 (above), but there are another 34 antique suites facing the Kremlin. The restaurant Moskovsky (T 258 7068) has won awards for its Russian-European menu, devised by a French chef. *Mokhovaya Ulitsa 15/1, T 258 7000, www.national.ru*

Golden Apple

Designed by the Canadian Rafael Shafir and opened in 2004, the 92-room Golden Apple was the first boutique hotel in the city. Occupying a 19th-century building near the Hermitage Gardens, you can't miss the huge, gold, apple-shaped sofa glinting in its window. The rest of Shafir's interiors are more understated, and were quite a departure for Moscow at that time. A colour scheme distinguishes each of the residential floors, and this is continued in the detailing in the rooms, such as the orange touches in this Superior Room (above). The Apple Bar is atypical for Moscow too, being half lobby and half DJ bar. Sushi and tapas are served alongside caipirinhas and margaritas while Fashion TV plays on the plasma screen.
Malaya Dmitrovka Ulitsa 11, T 980 7000, www.goldenapple.ru

Ararat Park Hyatt

With 20 of its 220 rooms being luxury suites, the Ararat Park is where many an American pop star stays while touring in Moscow – perhaps you could join them in an impromptu karaoke session if you reserve a Park Executive Suite (above). Excellently located beside the Bolshoi Theatre (see p032) and Tretyakovsky Proezd (see p080), the hotel takes its name from the Soviet-Armenian eaterie that previously occupied the building. That legendary restaurant's legacy is upheld in the hotel's ground-floor Café Ararat (see p062), but the most visually spectacular of the five restaurants here is the 10th-floor Conservatory Lounge and Bar, which has a glass roof and superb views of the city. At the Quantum Health Club, you can take a dip in the pool (right) or make use of the gym and spa facilities. *Neglinnaya Ulitsa 4, T 783 1234, moscow.park.hyatt.com*

MaMaison Pokrovka Suite Hotel

British firm Jestico + Whiles designed the interiors for Moscow's first all-suite hotel. Chic rooms have kitchenettes, sink-into sofas, parquet floors, plasma TVs and a sexy scarlet-red and pastel colour scheme. We'd recommend a One Bedroom Deluxe or the 161 sq m Presidential Suite (right), with its cheeky bedside bath for a post-clubbing, champagne-charged dip. The restaurant Numbers (above) was designed by young St Petersburg architect Anton Gorlanov, who has created a kitsch but refined space: walls are etched with numerals, and giant gold bauble lamps add an art deco touch, while chef Said Fadli serves up Russian and European dishes. The Tezon Bar excels not in vodka, but tequila, and ceiling lights are fashioned from upturned bottles. Appropriately for Pokrovka's Clean Ponds location, there's also a luxe spa and pool.
Pokrovka Ulitsa 40/2, T 229 5757, www.pokrovka-moscow.com

Swissotel Krasnye Holmy

The tallest structure in the new Riverside Towers business district was designed by Yuri Gnedovsky – the president of the Union of Russian Architects – and is a rather frightening example of current tastes in official architecture. However, ugly as the kitschy steel-and-glass tower may be, its steepled 170m gives panoramic views from all of the 235 rooms and suites. But perhaps the best spot from which to enjoy them is through the floor-to-ceiling windows of the City Space Bar and Lounge (above) on the 34th floor, in what looks like a UFO plonked on top of the building. Next door is the pressure-cooker-shaped Moscow International Performing Arts Center (T 730 1011), which stages classical music, jazz and ballet performances. *Kosmodamianskaya Naberezhnaya 52/6, T 787 9800, www.swissotel.com/moscow*

Metropol Hotel

In Soviet times, this was the finest place to stay in Moscow. Built in the fashionable art nouveau style, the hotel was opened in 1901; the decoration was by the best Russian painters of the 20th century, Konstantin Korovin and Mikhail Vrubel, with some gorgeous mosaic murals by the latter. The hotel's history is equally as rich: it has seen Rasputin debauch, Chaliapin sing and Lenin, Stalin and Trotsky meet.

The listed building's interiors are well preserved and 72 of its 362 rooms are deluxe, with fine period details, including the Presidential Suites (Room 2264, above), which have hosted Jacques Chirac, Al Gore and Juan Carlos of Spain. The restaurant Metropol (T 270 1061), with its glass dome and marble fountain, is the hotel's best. *Teatralny Proezd 1/4, T 501 7800, www.metropol-moscow.ru*

The Ritz-Carlton
On the Red Square site of the demolished Intourist Hotel, The R-C is a 'Luzhkov-style' classic, although it was designed by the brutalist Andrei Meerson (see p068), with interiors by Peter Silling. Opened in 2007 at a cost of £180m, the extravagance is hard to beat – its spa covers 2,000 sq m; the ballroom holds 700; its sushi comes garnished with gold leaf; and the Tsar's Breakfast (Cristal, Kobe beef, truffle omelette) costs £350. The 334 rooms are the most spacious in the city, and are done out in dark cherry and burl wood with bathrooms in marble from the Altay Mountains, while the 237 sq m Ritz-Carlton Suite has full-height windows overlooking the Kremlin and Russian imperial-style furnishings. The O2 Lounge (right) is a top-floor DJ bar topped with a glass dome; Meerson's tribute to his modernist past.
Tverskaya Ulitsa 3, T 225 8888, www.ritzcarlton.com

Baltschug Kempinski

The word *baltschug* is Tartarian and translates as 'mud'. This unprepossessing name derives from the low-lying road used by the Tartars in their raids on Moscow in the Middle Ages, and on which the hotel is situated. The Kempinski opened in 1992 and is essentially a respectable business hotel run by a creative team. Of the 230 rooms, the best are the three suites given a bespoke touch in 2007, redesigned by David Linley, the Swedish company Living Design (right) and Princess Michael of Kent. If you want stunning views of the Kremlin, opt for its namesake suite (above). The hotel has five restaurants and bars – Bar Baltschug boasts a vodka sommelier, who ought to change the mind of anyone who remains convinced that Russia's favourite (and cheapest) tipple is simply flavourless firewater. Especially after four or five shots.
Balchug Ulitsa 1, T 230 5500, www.kempinski-moscow.com

Historical Hotel Sovietsky

An example of the pompous architectural style of the Stalin era, the Sovietsky was finished in 1952. The current owners have opted to emphasise rather than conceal, adding to the Soviet-era features with a red banner on the rooftop, hammers and sickles, portraits of Lenin and red carpets on the marble staircases. For the full-on experience, reserve one of the Signature Suites (such as Stalin's Apartment), where everything – with the exception of an up-to-date bathroom – parodies totalitarian chic. Standard rooms are less impressive. The kitsch of Restaurant Yar (above), with its original frescoes and crystal chandelier, is the perfect backdrop for a trashy nightly cabaret about Rasputin, featuring dancing gypsies and Tropicana-style costumes. *Leningradsky Prospekt 32/2, T 960 2000, www.sovietsky.ru*

24 HOURS

SEE THE BEST OF THE CITY IN JUST ONE DAY

Assuming that you've already seen the obvious tourist sights – the Kremlin (see po12), the cathedrals and Lenin's Mausoleum (Red Square, T 623 5527), which architect Aleksei Schusev modelled on Babylonian ziggurats and where you can visit the embalmed corpse of the Revolutionary leader – there are plenty more must-sees in one of the world's great capitals.

The New Tretyakov Gallery (Krymsky Val 10, T 230 7788) has a huge collection of Russian avant-garde art and the Contemporary History Museum (Tverskaya Ulitsa 21, T 699 6724) includes a quaint display of comrades' gifts to Soviet potentates. Moscow's rapid expansion has engulfed its former aristocratic villas, and some are now museums in parks, such as Kuskovo (Ulitsa Yunosti 2, T 370 0160) and Ostankino (1-ya Ostankinskaya Ulitsa 5, T 683 4645).

But it's after dark that Muscovites really come out to play. Ballet at the Bolshoi (Teatralnaya Ploshchad 1, T 250 7317) is perennially popular, despite ongoing renovations to the main building. After you have taken in a performance, there's a bewildering choice of nightlife, such as the decadent club/restaurant Bon (see po39).

However, do plan ahead. Moscow is huge, its sights are spread out, the climate is harsh and traffic is gridlocked on weekdays. Take the stunning underground (see po34) or hire a limo (ask your concierge) – the only way to turn up to the latest opening party. *For full addresses, see Resources.*

10.00 Volkonsky Khleb

A pleasant stop-off for a light breakfast, this bakery, with its silk chairs and cosy tables, is probably the most Francophilic joint in town; the waiters even know how to say *enchanté*. An outlet of the French Maison Kayser patisserie chain, Volkonsky has brought back an almost forgotten slice of Moscow life – the neighbourhood bakery/café – and its shelves and counter are resplendent with a profusion of breads and baguettes, multicoloured éclairs, *macarons*, turnovers, sugared brioches and other dentally challenging treats, all freshly made on the premises. From here it's a short hop to Mayakovskaya (overleaf). *Bolshaya Sadovaya Ulitsa 46/2, T 299 3620, www.volkonsky.ru*

11.00 Mayakovskaya metro station
This is the most beautiful station on the Moscow underground, which is no mean feat, as the city's best craftsmen worked on this public transport project in the 1930s. Mayakovskaya architect Aleksei Dushkin's linear perspective wouldn't have been out of place in the Renaissance, but unfortunately it's been rather spoiled during a recent revamp. However, the chance to see the unique ceiling mosaics by Alexander Deyneka are worth at least 1,000 times the price of a ticket (0.25p). Mayakovskaya opened to commuters in 1938 and its platforms were used for government sessions during the siege of Moscow in 1941. Other stations were used as air-raid shelters, while the deep Arbatsky line that was built in the 1950s doubled as a series of nuclear bunkers. As a place of shelter in times of trouble, it certainly beats Charing Cross.
Triumfalnaya Ploshchad 4

13.00 Prado Cafe

From Mayakovskaya, take Line 2 and 7 on the metro to Kitai Gorod, for lunch at Prado. Interiors are opulent and typically New Russian – a clash of neo-baroque and classical references – yet executed with more taste than is found elsewhere in the city. There are fountains in the bathrooms, statues of eagles, a peacock sculpture embedded in one wall, columnar lights, statement chandeliers, dark woods and luxurious drapes. Swiss chef Peter-Paul Speckert oversees a mainly European and Asian menu – the risotto with veal fillet is recommended – and, as well as Moscow restaurants' ubiquitous sushi selection, there's a Peruvian ceviche bar. T.A.T.u sang at Prado's anniversary party, although presumably not in the VIP karaoke room. *Slavyanskaya Ploshchad 2, T 784 6969, www.prado-cafe.ru*

15.30 All-Russia Exhibition Centre (VVC)
This monumental expo park was erected to celebrate the economic achievements of the Soviet system. The flamboyant, Stalinist style of the 77 pavilions remains awesome; even more surprising is that some are still used as exhibition centres, while others house, ironically, wholesalers of imported goods. In the Armenia pavilion, you can taste superb local brandies, which go down rather well in winter; the 1960s Circular Panorama shows Communist-era documentaries; the magnificent colonnade of the Breeding Rabbits pavilion is rather over the top considering its function; and the Space Exploration pavilion is fronted by the Vostok rocket (above), in which Yuri Gagarin became the first man in space. You could easily spend an entire day here. *Estate 119, Mira Prospekt, T 544 3400, www.vvcentre.ru*

19.00 Winzavod

The 'Wine Factory' is a contemporary arts centre housed in a renovated 19th-century industrial complex. The former winery was overhauled by Russian architect and artist Alexander Brodsky, and the 20,000 sq m space, which opened in 2007, has become the hub of a burgeoning art scene – it hosted the Moscow Biennale in its three huge exhibition spaces, and the city's top galleries, such as Marat Guelman (T 228 1159), Aidan (see p062) and Regina (T 228 1330) have relocated here. The centre is still being developed, but is already home to artists' studios, cafés, bars and shops, such as the concept store Cara & Co (see p084). Events, from video installations and exhibition openings to festivals and gigs, take place here nearly every weekend.
4-ya Syromyatnichesky Pereulok 1/6, T 917 4646, www.winzavod.com

22.00 Bon

Like the two Bons in Paris, this restaurant was also designed by Philippe Starck, but here he has created a dark, decadent shrine to New Russian mafia-chic. If it were all meant to be satire – there are gold-plated Kalashnikovs for light fixtures, black sofas embroidered with golden skulls, eagle-topped thrones, mismatched cutlery, Gothic chandeliers, defaced frescoes and nihilist graffiti – it is lost on the beautiful creatures who flock here. Bon is now run by Arkady Novikov – Moscow's Terence Conran – who has revived the kitchen with a menu of international and Italian dishes, such as black cod with Miso sauce, venison ravioli, and homemade sorbets and breads, and also pumped up the sound system and added a dancefloor for a clubbier vibe.
Yakimanskaya Naberezhnaya 4/4/1,
T 737 8008, www.bonmoscow.ru

URBAN LIFE

CAFÉS, RESTAURANTS, BARS AND NIGHTCLUBS

Moscow has become one of the world's great nightlife capitals, and it gets livelier each year. It's as if the city's partygoers are making up for so much lost time under Communism. There are venues for all tastes – from hedonistic dance clubs awash with oligarch money (and those desperate for a cut of it) and high-design restaurant/bars with global-quality chefs to underground bohemian hangouts.

Self-indulgence is at its most brazen at destinations such as Rai (Bolotnaya Nabereznaya 9, T 767 1474), where the city's famous *feis kontrol* (door nazism) is at its most brutal. It's even harder to get in to Krysha Mira (Tarasa Shevchenko Naberezhnaya 2/3) in summer, thanks to its Ibiza-style terrace for dancing under the stars. Similar élitism can even exist at restaurants such as Gallery Art Cafe (see p057), so ask your concierge to reserve a table for you or put you on the guestlist (neither will guarantee entry, though), dress up to the nines and learn a few Russian pleasantries.

A new trend has been to mix genres, as venues try to be all things to all people. Solyanka (see p045) is a restaurant, club and boutique, and indie nightspot Justo Bain Douche (see p049) holds aesthetics lectures and stages theatre. In summer, party on boats cruising the Moskva or at a temporary beach club; in winter, events are held at ice rinks in the Hermitage Gardens (Ulitsa Karetny Ryad 3/7, T 747 8979) and the Young Pioneers Stadium (see p088). *For full addresses, see Resources.*

Suzy Wong Bar

The first stage in an ongoing conversion of a former textile factory into a cultural centre by artist Evgeny Mitta, this lounge bar holds regular exhibitions and concerts. Architecture and design offices have now moved in to the complex, and development is continuing through 2008. Suzy Wong is part Raffles hotel, part industrial chic, with a drawing-room ambience, one of the longest bars in Moscow and a fine Asian fusion menu, specialising in Chinese food and that Moscow obsession – sushi. Come here for its superbly good-value 'business' lunch, a clever way around the outrageous expense of eating out in this city, or for a chilled cocktail to kickstart your evening. *Timura Frunze Ulitsa 11/34, T 245 4849, www.suzywongbar.ru*

You Cafe

A good all-round option for day or night, this DJ café is perfect for an inexpensive afternoon snack, or come after dark to get revved up for a Moscow clubbing session. Two floors are connected by a wide wooden staircase and furnished with brown leather sofas, lacquered tables, oversized lampshades and ornamental gilding on the downstairs walls. Food is of the Franco/Italian bistro variety, with dishes such as Burgundy snails and cream of chestnut soup. The music policy is directed by You Cafe's founder, the well-connected Alexei Shcherbina, who invites along the city's favourite DJs, such as Sergei Sapunov, B-Voice, Maxim Zorkin and Anton Kubikov. The pre-party gets going around 9pm and starts winding down after 2am, when most revellers head for the clubs.
Pushechnaya Ulitsa 4, T 621 4907, www.youcafe.ru

Not So Far East

Capitalising on Moscow's appetite for Asian cuisine, Not So Far East (as the name suggests) is bringing it ever closer to 'home'. Sure, it's been done before, but Arkady Novikov pulls it off here with fewer gimmicks – the nearby Turandot (T 739 0011) serves up Chinese dishes in a mock 18th-century Versailles palace that cost £25m – and more finesse. The speciality Kamchatka crab is done any which way; other highlights coming out of the open kitchen include foie gras sushi, Kobe beef, and grapefruit sorbet with basil. Designed by Japanese firm Super Potato, there's the obligatory DJ lounge and chillout space, but also racks of bottles filled with oils and coloured water; tables made of tree trunks and a glass wall filled with cinnamon, pasta, chillies and bay leaves.
Tverskoy Bulvar 15/2, T 694 0641

Solyanka

In 2007, this multi-functional venue altered the course of Moscow nightlife. On week days, it is a restaurant with an eclectic international menu (chicken and mango quesadilla, beet vinaigrette, dorado, pig leg, but no *solyanka*, a Russian stew) and a boutique, selling European labels, inside a late 18th-century merchant's residence with creaky floorboards and mismatched furniture. But come 11pm at the weekend, it metamorphoses into a club, with the mandatory *feis kontrol*, as the volume is cranked up and the lighting cranked down. Thursday is the Flammable Beats' hip-hop night, Fridays see dance parties organised by DJs Anton Kubikov and Sergei Sapunov, and guest stars play on Saturdays. A steamy stew of another sort, then – and one that's not a bit like your mother used to make.
Solyanka 11/6, T 221 7557, s-11.ru

Maki Cafe

Rough concrete vaults, exposed brick walls and ducts, cheap wooden furniture – the 'under refurbishment' look is hot right now, and no one does it better than St Petersburg designer Andrei Dmitriev. Stylish and honest, Maki is a great alternative to the flashy and overpriced restaurants around Tverskaya. On weekdays, sit quietly with a laptop and a paper or come with friends to sample the superb-value Asian and international menu – highlights include sorrel soup, maki rolls (naturally), green salads, Thai coconut soup, duck in plum sauce, beef stroganoff and a great veggie selection. At the weekend, head downstairs to the chilled-out lounge, with flickering candles, inviting red sofas and a long bar and extensive cocktail list. Unobtrusive DJs spin soulful house and jazz.
Glinitchevsky Pereulok 3, T 292 9731

Gazgolder

Another club with an unusual location, in the disused Arma Plant gasworks built in the second half of the 19th century, Gazgolder is hidden in an industrial estate and until recently was one of the most exclusive venues in Moscow. Today, it's more accessible but hasn't lost its unique charm. This is a low-profile club, drawing an arty crowd into this pseudo-Gothic mansion, which with its chandeliers, roaring fire and skulls on the mantelpiece could be a set for *Tales of the Unexpected*. Uplifting tech-house and gloomy tribal fill the two dancefloors. The club is part of a large-scale project that comprises a record label, film studio and art gallery. *Nizhny Susalny Pereulok 5/2, T 226 3340, www.gazgolder.com*

Justo Bain Douche

Named after club/restaurant Les Bains Douches in Paris, as well as its location in a former *banya*, Justo opened in 2007 in the former Central Bathhouse. Running with its theme, tiles have been kept along with signs such as 'Comrades! Take good care of bath sheets' and novelty toilet chairs have been added. During the week, the stage is used for theatre and lectures on philosophy and aesthetics, the dancefloor for daytime ballet and yoga classes, and there's also a cinema. Club nights attract indie kids in tight jeans and ironic tees, bohos, artists, designers and fans of lounge, electro and bastard pop on Thursdays and the Freak Boutique parties at the weekend, complete with live show. Enter through an unmarked door down an alley. It's all very East Berlin.
Teatralny Proezd 3, T 625 6836

Sky Lounge

Take the lift up to the 22nd floor of the Academy of Sciences building (see p015), inside its 'golden brains', and the stunning, floor-length, teardrop chandelier that greets you is a foretaste of the luxury that lies within. Sky Lounge could easily rest on its laurels, assured of a clientele because of its breathtaking 360-degree city views, in summer from an outside terrace. Instead, amid a tasteful, colonial Asian-style décor, including a VIP tatami area, the restaurant serves up a diverse menu of international cuisines, with dishes such as herring carpaccio, beef stroganoff, barramundi in Thai sauce and a dessert of pineapple lasagne. On weekends, it doubles as a club with DJ sets. Be warned, though, the prices are as vertiginous as the location. *Academy of Sciences, Leninsky Prospekt 32a, T 938 5775, www.skylounge.ru*

Ikra Club
The quality and intimacy of the eclectic club nights and gigs here has won Ikra a host of awards. Bands could be well known or underground; dance parties feature name DJs or celebs; the music policy is across the board. The décor, by Denis Khomyak of St Petersburg's Rechniki, is all opium-den chic, pin-up art, trashy posters and gilded wallpaper.
Ulitsa Kazakova 8a, T 505 5351

The Apartment

Done out as a smart SoHo-style loft, the interior of this restaurant/bar is split into various open-plan 'rooms'. You know, like in a 'real' apartment. Sip a cocktail on the leather armchairs in the lounge; smoke a cigar beside the fire; watch films in the cinema room; listen to the pianist in the music area; and even take cooking lessons in the kitchen – after trying the food, you might be tempted. The Apartment's Russian chef spent 16 years in Paris, and combines strong French flavours with a nouvelle cuisine-style approach, with each plate, such as smoked trout and broccoli salad or veal in mushroom sauce, delicately presented. Downstairs, there's a wine boutique, with more than 2,500 labels. So, make yourself at home. A soak in the gorgeous claw-foot bath might, however, be overstaging your welcome.
Savinskaya Naberezhnaya 21, T 518 6060, www.the-apartment.ru

Gallery Art Cafe

A flagship venue of Arkady Novikov, Gallery attracts glamour like a magnet. Pop stars, TV moguls and the new breed of Russian mafia – club door controllers – and their model girls flood this 24-hour restaurant and lounge every weekend from 10pm; in summer, a couch-strewn courtyard eases the squeeze. Gallery justifies its lofty name with photo exhibitions and displays of iconic magazine covers, illuminated among the dark furniture and brown and cream décor by theatre spotlights. Italian chef William Lamberti keeps the global cuisine simple, concentrating on seasonal ingredients and stand-alone flavours – pasta with black truffles, leg of lamb, wild strawberry soup – served here on a bed of lounge music and a side of eye candy. *Petrovka Ulitsa 27, T 790 1596, www.cafegallery.ru*

Fabrique

An unlikely resident of the Moscow State University of Design and Technology, this club was founded by graduates and attracts an attitude-free crowd. There have been collaborations with London's Turnmills, and sessions from Felix Da Housecat, Ibiza veterans such as Roger Sanchez, designer Karim Rashid (DJ Kreemy) and local DJs, who lord over the semi-circular dancefloor from the raised DJ platform, and rain down the full spectrum of house music. Upstairs is a chillout area featuring a transparent floor, sofas and curtained-off restaurant booths (above) for trysts over the mainly European menu with that hottie you just met on the dancefloor.
Kosmodamianskaya Naberezhnaya 2, T 540 9955, www.fabrique.ru

B1 Maximum
The biggest club in the city occupies
a former machine-tool factory and hosts
gigs by ageing rockers such as Iggy Pop,
Alice Cooper and Bryan Ferry, and local
talents t.A.T.u and GrOb, for crowds of up
to 3,500. The vast industrial space houses
a dancefloor and two balconies; VIP and
Super VIP areas. How very Moscow.
Ultisa Ordzhonikidze 11, T 648 6777,
www.b1arena.ru

INSIDER'S GUIDE

MIKHAIL ROZANOV, PHOTOGRAPHER AND ARTIST

Focusing on architecture, photographer and artist Mikhail Rozanov is represented by Aidan Gallery (4-ya Syromyatnichesky Pereulok 1/6, T 228 1158), one of the most prestigious in Moscow, and part of the burgeoning art and design scene at Winzavod (see p038). Rozanov's favourite coffee house is Cappuccino (Nikitsky Bulvar 12, T 290 1498), which he rates for its cosy atmosphere and friendly staff, and he also likes to drop in to the French Cafe (Smolenskaya Ploshchad 3, T 937 8424) for an early breakfast, or even a late-night snack, since, like many Moscow venues, it's open 24 hours.

When it comes to shopping, Rozanov favours two boutiques that offer hard-to-find brands – Le Form (see p083) and the recently opened Traffic+ (see p087). If he's pushed for time, he'll pop by Podium concept store (Novinsky Bulvar 18, T 202 4686), as it's situated around the corner from his apartment in Novy Arbat.

A connoisseur of dishes from Russia and the former Soviet states, Rozanov often books a table at the Russian Cuisine Room (Tverskoy Bulvar 10, T 692 0216) at Tass Club, which is run by the news agency; Genatsvale Restaurant (Ulitsa Novy Arbat 11/2, T 203 9453), which offers delicious Georgian cuisine in a rustic, intimate interior, or Ararat Café (Neglinnaya Ulitsa 4, T 783 1234), which specialises in Armenian food. For a big night out, Rozanov heads to restaurant/club Solyanka (see p045), where the chef is as talented as the DJs. *For full addresses, see Resources.*

Russian Cuisine Room,

ARCHITOUR

A GUIDE TO MOSCOW'S ICONIC BUILDINGS

Some critics speak of Moscow's stylistic diversity with admiration, others with displeasure, but the city is indisputably omnivorous when it comes to architecture. Its imperial picturesqueness and medieval radial plan were seen as a problem by the avant-garde in the 1920s and radicals even proposed pulling everything down and building anew. However, the moderates won out, and constructivist buildings were blended in with the old city centre.

Stalinist reconstruction reshaped the skyline, producing grand, stylistically homogeneous complexes, such as the Lomonosov Moscow State University (GSP-2, Leninsky Gory). Khrushchev is associated with the uncontrolled introduction of neomodernism and prefabricated panel construction. A monument to the times, the five-storey housing block became a Communist machine for living, while the Brezhnev era produced dormitory suburbs and superb neomodernist and brutalist structures, such as Velodrome Krylatskoye (see p094) and the Centipede building (see p068).

In the 1990s, Moscow's architecture was tainted by the Luzhkov style: historical replicas and buildings created to suit the whims of the incumbent mayor. Since the new millennium, the construction of the Moscow International Business Centre (see p010) and the realisation of buildings such as Copper House (opposite) have raised hopes that architectural common sense will win through. *For full addresses, see Resources.*

Boiler house, Kremlin Power Plant

Ivan Zholtovsky's professional biography is typical of an early 20th-century Russian architect. He began his career in the 1900s as a devoted follower of Andrea Palladio; in the 1920s, he joined the avant garde; and by the 1930s, he was an exponent of Stalinist neoclassicism. This doesn't mean that Zholtovsky was, in the words of Philip Johnson, a 'high-class whore' who changed styles like clients. He believed that his work was not rooted in historical styles but in principles of harmony, particularly in the case of industrial buildings, for which it was hard to find ancient counterparts. This 1927 boiler house – a product of so-called 'harmonised constructivism' – places new forms within classical rules of composition. Serving the Kremlin, it is the oldest power plant in Moscow, and is still operational. *Raushskaya Naberezhnaya 10*

Copper House

Sergei Skuratov is one of the few Russian architects who have been successful in spite of a culture generally antipathetic to contemporary architecture. The significance of this condominium block, completed in 2004, goes beyond the scope of a single person's work, and is a bright symbol of Moscow's architectural evolution: today's élite residence should not mimic, it should innovate. Exclusivity is suggested by the integrity of the building itself: the weathered copper façade, its articulated corbels and glass walls at each end, which are shielded from prying eyes by angled glazed blinds. However, Copper House does not dominate its surroundings; it enhances them, expanding the green wedge that spreads from Ulitsa Ostozhenka down to the Moskva river.

Butikovsky Pereulok 3

Centipede building

A fine example of Soviet brutalism, this 1978 apartment block was designed by Andrei Meerson. A massive slab is supported on a high trestle of cast-in-situ reinforced concrete, resting on the multifaceted 'legs' that give the building its nickname. The overlapping external wall panels, resembling Cyclopean scales, actually protect the joints from rainwater.
Begovaya Ulitsa 34

Penguin building

Brestskaya Ulitsa is not the best location in Moscow, being narrow and densely built-up with dull, inarticulate buildings. Faced with the common architectural dilemma that a new structure either has to merge in or stand out as confidently as possible, Ostozhenka Architects, led by Alexander Skokan, found the perfect solution for this office building – they just threw out the main façade. Clad in glass, it hangs above the street, reflecting the cars below, the clouds above and its neighbours on each side, uniting the sluggish architecture that surrounds it. Completed in 2004, it soon became a landmark, under different guises: architects call it the 'penguin', passers-by, the 'belly', and its inhabitants, the 'sail'.
1-ya Brestskaya Ulitsa 29

Melnikov's house

Hidden down a side street in Old Arbat, and squeezed between the neighbouring buildings, this house/studio is fascinating not because of its proportions or bizarre elegance, but because of the ingenuity of its architecture. Konstantin Melnikov's three-storey house, finished in 1929, comprises two interlocking cylinders: one contains the entrance hall and living room, while the taller one includes the kitchen, the bedroom and a top-floor studio. The honeycomb design not only saved on bricks, which were scarce at the time, but also made the walls more stable. Another innovation was the membrane ceiling, made up of two layers of board in a grid, requiring no supporting columns or girders. Since Melnikov's son died in 2006, the future of the house has been uncertain. *Krivoarbatsky Pereulok 6*

Zuyev Workers' Club

One of the main aims of constructivism was to invent new types of building for the collective socialist lifestyle. This resulted in the emergence of communal houses, kitchen-factories and workers' clubs, where the proletariat were supposed to spend their leisure time. Apart from Konstantin Melnikov, whose workers' clubs are well-known, one of the chief innovators in this field was Ilya Golosov. Zuyev, which was completed in 1928, is a brilliant work of technical aesthetics. The glazed cylinder that reveals the main staircase acts as a kind of driveshaft for the whole building, which amazingly still functions as a recreation centre today. No one remembers Zuyev, after whom the club was named, but the structure itself remains a must-see for visiting archi-buffs.
Lesnaya Ulitsa 18

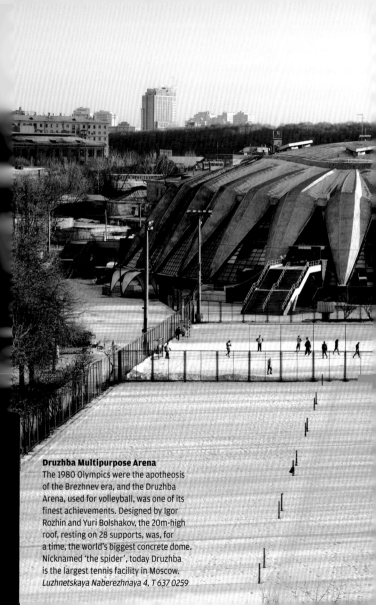

Druzhba Multipurpose Arena
The 1980 Olympics were the apotheosis
of the Brezhnev era, and the Druzhba
Arena, used for volleyball, was one of its
finest achievements. Designed by Igor
Rozhin and Yuri Bolshakov, the 20m-high
roof, resting on 28 supports, was, for
a time, the world's biggest concrete dome.
Nicknamed 'the spider', today Druzhba
is the largest tennis facility in Moscow.
Luzhnetskaya Naberezhnaya 4, T 637 0259

Tsentrosoyuz building

Many leaders of the avant-garde came to Russia to work – German architects Erich Mendelsohn and Ernst May designed a factory in Leningrad and an industrial settlement in Magnitogorsk respectively, while Le Corbusier proposed three projects for Moscow: the Tsentrosoyuz building (in collaboration with Pierre Jeanneret and Nikolaï Kolli), the doomed Palace of the Soviets and a redevelopment of the entire city (he suggested pulling down everything save the Kremlin and Kitai Gorod, and starting again). In the end, only Tsentrosoyuz (Central Union of Cooperative Societies) was realised, from 1928 to 1936. Today, it houses the Russian State Committee for Statistics. Although the interiors have been replaced, it is the best preserved monument of the interwar architectural avant-garde in Moscow.
Myasnitskaya Ulitsa 39

House on Embankment

Boris Iofan's 1931 housing complex was the crowning glory of the constructivist approach to communal living, and boasts a three-storey department store, a club and a cinema. Its 500 luxury flats, given to party members and the cultural élite, were hardly in keeping with Communist ideology, and are still among the most expensive properties in the whole city.
Bersenevskaya Naberezhnaya 20/2

SHOPPING

THE BEST RETAIL THERAPY AND WHAT TO BUY

Muscovites love to shop and do it with gusto, paying no attention to the sky-high prices; in fact, for many, the prices themselves, and the 'status' that being able to afford them brings, are the lure. The principal source of luxury and labels is the Mercury Company; its main outlets are on Tretyakovsky Proezd, which boasts Bentley, Dolce & Gabbana and Brioni, and at massive shopping complex Barvikha Luxury Village (Rublevo-Uspenskoe Shosse 114, T 980 6804), in Moscow's richest suburb. Traditional department store TsUM (Petrovka 2, T 933 7300) now boasts international brands, while the former state store GUM (3 Red Square, T 788 4343) is closer to a high-end mall, with Dior and MaxMara outlets. There are yet more boutiques on Tverskaya Ulitsa and the pedestrianised Stoleshnikov Pereulok, including Vivienne Westwood (No 9, T 624 3925) and fashion designer Denis Simachev's Store-bar (No 12/2, T 629 8085), where his signature Soviet kitsch runs riot.

If you're after Russian delicacies, such as caviar, fish and vodka, head to Yeliseyevsky (Tverskaya Ulitsa 14, T 209 4643), where you will find not only food but a stunning art nouveau interior. More tasty morsels are on offer at its rival, Globus-Gourmet (Ulitsa Bolshaya Yakimanka 22, T 995 2170). For local curios and unusual mementoes, head to Izmailovo Park for Vernisazh (Izmailovskoye Shosse 73), Moscow's only equivalent of an upscale flea market. *For full addresses, see Resources.*

Respublica

The brainchild of Russian sausage king Vadim Dymov, this flagship Respublica store is not your usual bookshop – it's more of a lifestyle boutique, its shelves stacked with art and coffee-table books, design objects and toys for grown-ups. Dymov, who sometimes works the tills, says: 'The principle is simple – we don't sell anything square.' A fine selection of books, techno gadgets, records, phones, work by Moscow artists, designer undies, creative stationery and American Apparel tees are displayed among the brightly coloured furniture. You can listen to CDs before you buy, there's a reading café and even a cinema. Open 24 hours, you'd have to be a particularly stubborn penny-pincher to leave here without buying something. *1st Tverskaya-Yamskaya 10, T 251 6527, www.respublica.ru*

Emperor Moth

This boutique is easy to spot: its windows are festooned with bare bulbs, dressing-room-style, and emblazoned with the slogan *Chic, blesk, krasota* ('The flashier, the better'). Look closer and you'll see a mannequin lounging in a snow-white bath and a plastic ceiling resembling a B-movie alien invasion. Designer/owner Katya Gomiashvili shot to fame with her hand-painted sheepskin coats, and has created a range of sneakers for Diadora. Alongside fellow CIS labels Arsenicum, Konstantin Gayday and Serguei Teplov, Gomiashvili's Emperor Moth collection features embroidered velour cardigans, beaded and pailletted sweatshirts, and tight-fitting tracksuit trousers and zip-up tracksuit tops with intricate appliqué. *Malaya Bronnaya Ulitsa 16, T 290 3888, www.emperormoth.com*

Le Form

This is the second, more spacious branch of one of the best multi-brand shops in Moscow, located just behind the Bolshoi Theatre – the original is further out in Novy Arbat. Le Form sells high-quality clothes by Russian fashion designers, such as Nina Donis, Oleg Biryukov and Svetlana Tegin, as well as the international brands Veronique Branquinho, Dries Van Noten, Nicole Farhi, Martin Margiela and Comme des Garçons, and is known for its generous discounts. Beautifully presented cabinets display sunglasses, accessories and hard-to-find perfumes by Il Profumo, Molinard and Sahlini, while one room is devoted to tableware, wooden toys and books.
Dmitrovsky Pereulok 7, T 660 0280, www.leform.ru

Cara & Co
Calling itself Moscow's first concept store, Cara & Co's arty, brick-walled space is divided into four zones: Fashion, with designers Akira Isogawa, Rick Owens, Ksubi and Natan; Vintage, for 1920s Bakelite bags to 1960s Lanvin pieces; Lifestyle, for books, mags, CDs and wine; and Break, a café and exhibition space.
Winzavod, 4-ya Syromyatnichesky Pereulok 1/8, T 223 4100, caraandco.com

Massandra

Dessert wines are the third pillar of the holy trinity of classic Russian drinks: the first two being Stolichnaya vodka and Armenian brandy. The Massandra winery in the Crimea, founded by Nicholas II in 1894, has collected around 150 awards for its wines at international tasting events, and it is said to have one of the largest selections of labels in the world. The last Russian tsar was very partial to fortified Livadia wine and always carried a flask with him. In this Moscow outlet, you can find excellent bottles of almost any vintage, whether your preference is for 2005 or 1905. The 1907 White Muscat No 35, the 1908 Pedro Massandra and even the tsar's darling, the 1918 Livadia (the year he passed away), are exceptional.
Ulitsa Oktiabrskaya 5, T 284 5757, www.agora-group.ru

Traffic+

At first sight, it seems that all the clothing in Traffic+ is very similar – black, white or grey. But that is an illusion; each item is unique and snapped up by a mostly arty and media-savvy clientele. Most of the 40 or so international clothing, accessories and design brands sold here cannot be found elsewhere in Moscow, such as the Paris- and New York-based Surface To Air label, which claims to produce anything 'from a telescope to a pin' and the French/German duo Bless, responsible for fur wigs and a vacuum-cleaner chair that was shown in the Centre Pompidou. The store's interior is littered with objets trouvés, such as old factory lamps, a 1950s counter, 1920s dolls and a 110cm birdcage; tables and mirror frames are fashioned from barn doors. *Chistoprudny Bulvar 21/2, T 621 4859, www.traffictraffic.ru*

SPORTS AND SPAS
WORK OUT, CHILL OUT OR JUST WATCH

Sport in Russia, together with ballet and space exploration, has always been political. In 1928, the constructivist Dinamo Stadium (Leningradsky Prospekt 36/1, T 612 7092) was built, as part of an unrealised project to stage a socialist Olympics, and was the biggest in Europe at the time. It's now home to two of Moscow's five football teams and hosts ice hockey in winter. Luzhniki Sports Complex (Luzhnetskaya Naberezhnaya 24, T 785 9717) opened in the 1950s and was a venue for the 1980 Olympics. The most distinguished addition for the Games was the Velodrome Krylatskoye (see p094). If you fancy a kickabout, good football pitches can be found in Luzhniki, and the main stadium can be hired out; perhaps one of Roman Abramovich's scouts will be watching.

In winter, Moscow is famous for its outdoor ice rinks. The best is at the Young Pioneers Stadium (Leningradsky Prospekt 31, T 613 0239), where you can skate to a DJ soundtrack. Gorki Park (Ulitsa Krymsky Val 9) offers tracks for speed skating. If you've always fancied taking a dip while it's snowing, then brave it with the locals at the heated outdoor Chaika Swimming Pool (opposite). In the 1990s, fitness clubs and health spas opened in the city. Among the best are World Class (Zhitnaya Ulitsa 14/2, T 771 6600) and Olympic Star (Rublevskoye Shosse 10, T 730 0300). For a traditional Russian *banya* (bathhouse), Sanduny (see p092) can't be bettered. *For full addresses, see Resources.*

Chaika Swimming Pool

A recent renovation has given Chaika, Moscow's first lido, which opened in 1957, a gym, a sauna, tennis courts, a mini-golf course and even dance classes, turning it into a true sports complex. Until the mid-1990s, its major rival was Moskva (a circular 130m-diameter outdoor pool built into the foundations of the Palace of the Soviets), but since the rebuilding of the Cathedral of Christ the Saviour, Chaika is again *the* place to take a dip – you could be treading water with the city's élite as well-known actors and politicians mingle here without ceremony. The pool is even used in winter – take the plunge after a sauna and swim as the snow is falling for a unique Moscow experience. In summer, part of the terrace is converted into a small beach, which is probably more tempting.
3-ya Turchaninov Pereulok 1/3, T 246 1344

Lokomotiv Stadium

The first single-purpose football stadium in Russia was built in 2002 to a design by Andrei Bokov, and once bore the name of 'Stalinets' (The Stalinist). Today, it is the home of Lokomotiv Moscow Football Club. The 28,800-capacity stadium is one of the best in the city, both in terms of its facilities and architecture. Despite its impressive dimensions, the structure doesn't look bulky. From the outside, it's hard to imagine that the white cables fixed to the four corner masts support an awning over the stands inside. The masts also have a decorative function: they are shaped like the Russian letter 'L', for Lokomotiv.
Bolshaya Cherkizovskaya 125,
eng.fclm.ru

Sanduny Bath House

The oldest *banya* in Moscow was founded in the early 1800s by the court actor Sila Sandunov, and set the standard across Russia. The present bathhouse was built in 1896 on the original site and it is beautifully preserved. Viennese architect Boris Freidenberg decorated this three-storey shrine to cleanliness with elements of baroque, Renaissance, Gothic, rococo, classical and Moorish styles. Marble was brought from Italy and Norway, floor tiles from England, Germany and Switzerland, and there are exquisite frescoes, statues, mosaics, chandeliers and stained-glass windows. Bathing is unisex, and you can also get a haircut, massage, mani or pedi. For the full Russian experience, hit yourself with *vennik* (birch twigs) in the sauna. *Neglinnaya Ulitsa 14/3-7, T 625 4631, www.sanduny.ru*

Velodrome Krylatskoye

Built for the 1980 Moscow Olympics, the Velodrome Krylatskoye is located beside the Moskva in the picturesque Tatarovsky Hills district and, thanks to the organic nature of its design, sits in harmony with its surroundings. The building, designed by Soviet architect Natalia Voronina, is a 168m-long oval-shaped structure with two grandstands, seating 6,000 people. Its aesthetic appeal lies in the compound roof – a hyperbolic paraboloid supported by two sloping arcs. Resembling a resting butterfly, the structure has a similarity to those of the Japanese architect Kenzo Tange. The 333.33m Siberian larchwood cycle track is one of the fastest ever built, with 13 world records to its name. The multipurpose venue is also used for mini-football, handball and athletics.
Krylatskaya Ulitsa 10, T 140 7270

ESCAPES

WHERE TO GO IF YOU WANT TO LEAVE TOWN

The Moscow Region covers an area larger than Belgium, Denmark or Switzerland, and is full of interesting sights, in varying degrees of preservation and remoteness from the metropolis. Before the 1917 Revolution, there were many noblemen's estates around the city. Some have since been absorbed by its urban sprawl and others destroyed. However, Arkhangelskoe (see p102) is an exception; the estate has been well preserved and meticulously restored. To the west of the city, along the Rublevo-Uspenskoe Highway, are the suburbs of Barvikha and Zhukovka; this is where the new money lives. The high fences hide some fine examples of contemporary architecture, which is scarce in Moscow. Here you'll also find Barvikha Luxury Village (see p080), a shopping complex and cultural centre designed by the Moscow firm Proekt Meganom.

North of the city lies a chain of reservoirs that forms part of the Moscow Canal linking the Moskva to the Volga and, ultimately, the Black Sea, the Baltic, the Caspian and the White Sea. This waterway is a fine route for a scenic boat ride, which starts from the North River Terminal (Leningradskoe Highway 51, T 221 7222). Accessible both by water and the Ostashkovskoe Highway is the stylish Pirogovo Resort, which boasts a yacht club, tennis courts, riding stables and several restaurants, including Kot Dazur (see p100), all situated on the shores of the Klyazma Reservoir.
For full addresses, see Resources.

Lenin Museum, Gorki Leninsky

This addition to the Lenin Museum – a grandiose building containing exhibition sites and conference halls – was built in 1987 on the Gorki estate (the place where Lenin died), shortly before the collapse of the USSR. Designed by Leonid Pavlov, it combines a simplicity of method, similar to that used in minimalist architecture, with the solemnity of a mausoleum. 'At the end of my life, I've built the Parthenon,' said Pavlov. The main exhibition features Soviet technologies of the mid-1980s, such as holographic projections, moving dioramas and films that portray Lenin as if he were still alive. You can also visit his former residence, an 1830s manor complex that was renovated by art nouveau architect Fyodor Shekhtel in 1909. It's 11km south-east of the outer ring road. *T 548 9309*

Lenin Museum, Gorki Leninsky

Kot Dazur, Pirogovo Resort
The Pirogovo Resort is the city's version
of the French Riviera, with villas, yachts,
eateries and seasonal contemporary
art fairs clustered around the mirror-
like waters of the Klyazma Reservoir.
Restaurant Kot Dazur serves top-quality
Mediterranean cuisine, its name being
a Russian transliteration of Côte d'Azur.
Klyazminskoe Vodokhranilishche 3,
T 588 8314, www.kotdazur.ru

Arkhangelskoe

'Have you been to Arkhangelskoe? If not, you should go there!', insisted the Russian writer Alexander Herzen in 1833. The estate, purchased in 1810 by Prince Nicholai Yusupov 'for merrymaking, not for profit', was recommended even by French city guides of the 19th century as a place that all visitors to Moscow should see. A classical architectural ensemble, with multi-level Italian gardens and a beautiful park, where aristocrats and emperors spent their leisure time, it is well preserved and still plays a major role as a social and cultural attraction. The Arkhangelskoe museum displays a fine collection of 18th-century paintings and the Gonzaga Theatre holds classical and jazz music festivals and social events. There is also a sanatorium on the estate, which offers a variety of treatments. *Ilinskoe Shosse 5km, T 363 1375, www.arkhangelskoe.ru*

NOTES
SKETCHES AND MEMOS

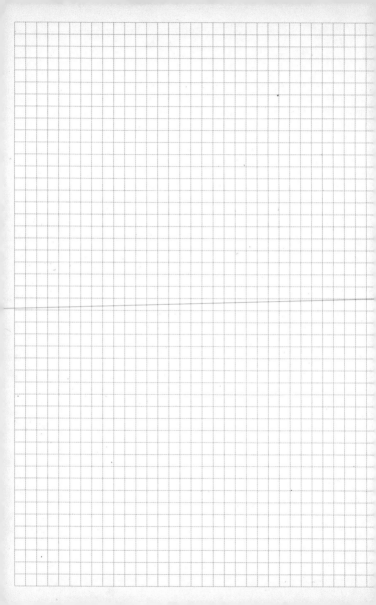

RESOURCES
CITY GUIDE DIRECTORY

A

Academy of Sciences 015
Leninsky Prospekt 32a
T 938 0309

Aidan Gallery 062
Winzavod
4-ya Syromyatnichesky Pereulok 1/6
T 228 1158
www.aidan-gallery.ru

All-Russia Exhibition Centre (VVC) 037
Estate 119
Mira Prospekt
T 544 3400
www.vvcentre.ru

The Apartment 054
Savinskaya Naberezhnaya 21
T 518 6060
www.the-apartment.ru

Ararat Café 062
Ararat Park Hyatt
Neglinnaya Ulitsa 4
T 783 1234
www.moscow.park.hyatt.com

Arkhangelskoe 102
Ilinskoe Shosse 5km
T 363 1375
www.arkhangelskoe.ru

B

B1 Maximum Club 060
Ulitsa Ordzhonikidze 11
T 648 6777
www.b1arena.ru

Barvikha Luxury Village 080
Rublevo-Uspenskoe Shosse 114
8km
T 980 6804

Bolshoi Theatre 032
Teatralnaya Ploshchad 1
T 250 7317
www.bolshoi.ru/en

Bon 039
Yakimanskaya Naberezhnaya 4/4/1
T 737 8008
www.bonmoscow.ru

C

Cappuccino 062
Nikitsky Bulvar 12
T 290 1498

Cara & Co 084
Winzavod
4-ya Syromyatnichesky Pereulok 1/8
T 223 4100
caraandco.com

Centipede building 068
Begovaya Ulitsa 34

Chaika Swimming Pool 089
3-ya Turchaninov Pereulok 1-3
T 246 1344

Copper House 065
Butikovsky Pereulok 3

Contemporary History Museum 032
Tverskaya Ulitsa 21
T 699 6724
www.sovr.ru

D

Denis Simachev Store-bar 080
Stoleshnikov Pereulok 12/2
T 629 8085
www.denissimachev.com

Dinamo Stadium 088
Leningradsky Prospekt 36/1
T 612 7092
www.fcdynamo.ru

Druzhba Multipurpose Arena 074
Luzhnetskaya Naberezhnaya 4
T 637 0259

HOTELS

ADDRESSES AND ROOM RATES

Ararat Park Hyatt Moscow 020
Room rates:
double, from 25,400RUB;
Luxury Suite, from 52,800RUB;
Park Executive Suite, from 62,500RUB
Neglinnaya Ulitsa 4
T 783 1234
moscow.park.hyatt.com

Baltschug Kempinski 028
Room rates:
double, from 33,000RUB;
Design Suite, from 48,000RUB;
Kremlin Suite, from 73,000RUB
Balchug Ulitsa 1
T 230 5500
www.kempinski-moscow.com

Hotel Cosmos 016
Room rates:
double, 6,100RUB
Prospekt Mira 150
T 234 1000
www.hotelcosmos.ru

Enigma WEL 016
Room rates:
double, from 7,700RUB
Staraya Basmannaya Ulitsa 12/1
T 648 9292
www.wel-hotels.ru/enigma-wel-hotels-resorts.html

Golden Apple 018
Room rates:
double, 17,700 RUB;
Superior Room, 11,700RUB
Malaya Dmitrovka Ulitsa 11
T 980 7000
www.goldenapple.ru

Historical Hotel Sovietsky 030
Room rates:
double, 7,200 RUB;
Stalin's Apartment, 25,600RUB
Leningradsky Prospekt 32/2
T 960 2000
www.sovietsky.ru

MaMaison Pokrovka Suite Hotel 022
Room rates:
double, from 12,000RUB;
One Bedroom Deluxe Suite,
from 18,000RUB;
Presidential Suite, from 60,200RUB
Pokrovka Ulitsa 40/2
T 229 5757
www.pokrovka-moscow.com

Metropol Hotel 025
Room rates:
double, from 13,400RUB;
Deluxe Room, from 47,700RUB;
Presidential Suite, from 63,700RUB
Teatralny Proezd 1/4
T 501 7800
www.metropol-moscow.ru

The Ritz-Carlton 026
Room rates:
double, from 23,000RUB;
Ritz-Carlton Suite, from 509,000RUB
Tverskaya Ulitsa 3
T 225 8888
www.ritzcarlton.com

Le Royal Méridien National 017
Room rates:
double, 18,800RUB;
Kremlin Suite, 51,700RUB;
National Suite, 87,100RUB;
Presidential Suite, 97,700RUB
Mokhovaya Ulitsa 15/1
T 258 7000
www.national.ru

Swissotel Krasnye Holmy 024
  Room rates:
  double, from 11,400RUB
  Kosmodamianskaya Naberezhnaya 52/6
  T 787 9800
  www.swissotel.com/moscow

WALLPAPER* CITY GUIDES

Editorial Director
Richard Cook

Art Director
Loran Stosskopf
City Editor
Sergei Kulikov
Associate Writer
Jeremy Case
Editor
Rachael Moloney
Executive
Managing Editor
Jessica Firmin
Travel Bookings Editor
Sara Henrichs

Chief Designer
Daniel Shrimpton
Designer
Lara Collins
Map Illustrator
Russell Bell

Photography Editor
Christopher Lands
Photography Assistant
Robin Key

Sub-Editor
Stephen Patience
Editorial Assistant
Ella Marshall

Interns
Nicky Ashwell
Rosa Bertoli
Francesca Wilson

Wallpaper* Group
Editor-in-Chief
Tony Chambers
Publisher
Neil Sumner

Contributors
Alexandra Grigorieva
Mikhail Kotomin
Yana Melkumova
Ekaterina Melnikova
Robert Michaelis
Philip Mironov
Elisaveta Plavinskaya
Meirion Pritchard
Ellie Stathaki
Ilya Sverdlov
Ivan Tretiakov

Wallpaper* ® is a
registered trademark
of IPC Media Limited

All prices are correct at
time of going to press,
but are subject to change.

PHAIDON

Phaidon Press Limited
Regent's Wharf
All Saints Street
London N1 9PA

Phaidon Press Inc
180 Varick Street
New York, NY 10014

Phaidon® is a registered
trademark of Phaidon
Press Limited

www.phaidon.com

First published 2008
© 2008 IPC Media Limited

ISBN 978 0 7148 4748 1

A CIP Catalogue record for
this book is available from
the British Library.

Printed in China

PHOTOGRAPHERS

MOSCOW
A COLOUR-CODED GUIDE TO THE HOT 'HOODS

KITAI GOROD
Moscow's bling shopping quarter is also home to the art nouveau Hotel Metropol

CHISTYE PRUDY
The Clean Ponds area provides pleasant respite; the former KGB HQ is more chilling

NOVY ARBAT
Don't miss the residential architecture of the Golden Mile or Arbat's bohemian alleyways

KREMLIN
Russia's historical heart is a walled city of churches and imposing government buildings

TVERSKAYA
This area teems with bars, restaurants and nightlife options, notably the Bolshoi Theatre

ZAMOSKVORECHIE
South of the river, the old merchants' quarter is filled with onion domes and art galleries

For a full description of each neighbourhood, see the Introduction.
Featured venues are colour-coded, according to the district in which they are located.